I0171543

GOD

WHAT IS MY CALLING?

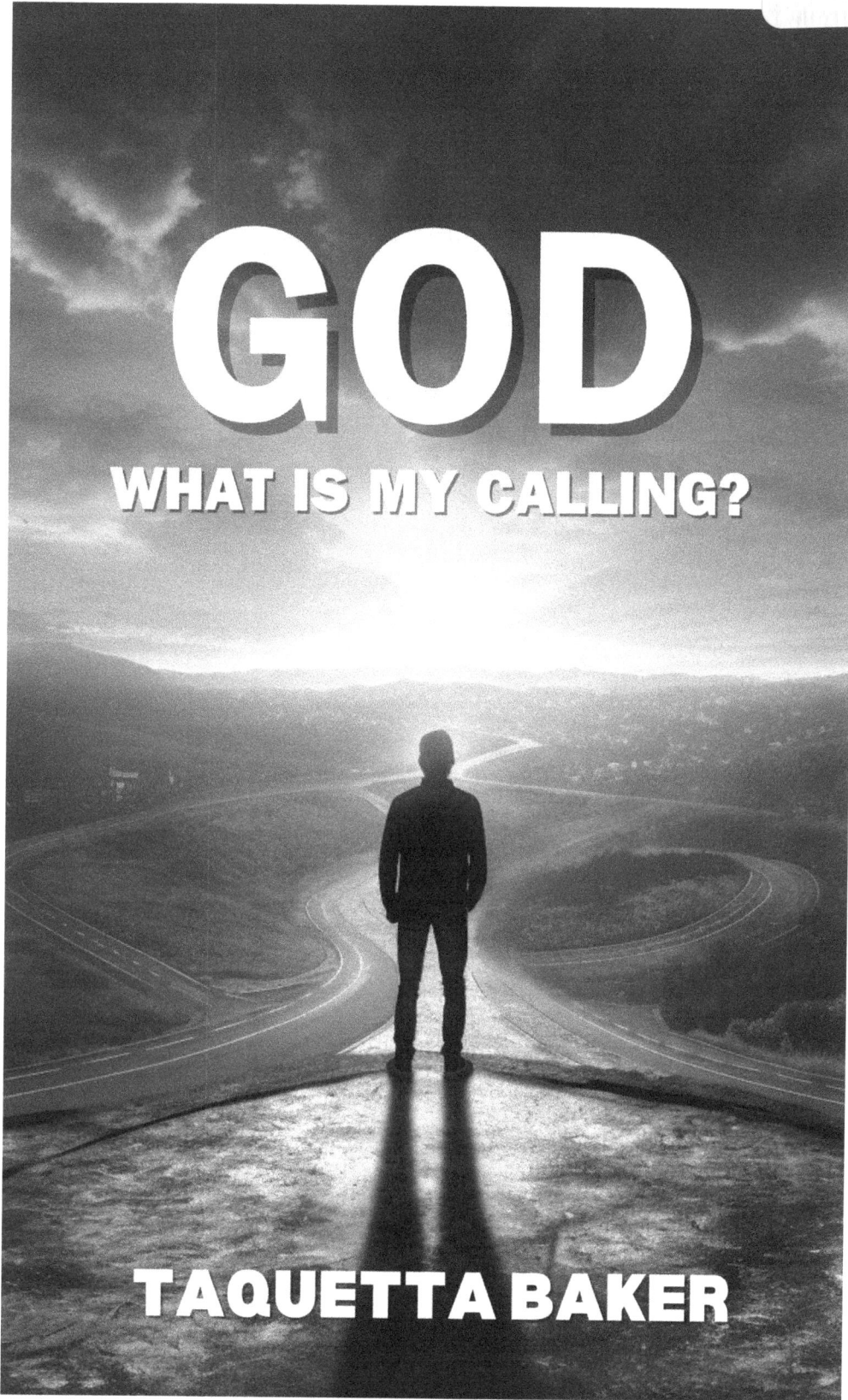

TAQUETTA BAKER

Kingdom Wellness Counseling and Mentoring Center

Christian Counseling

Ebook Products

GOD WHAT IS MY CALLING

Dr. TAQUETTA BAKER

Amazon Publications
Muncie, IN

Kingdom Wellness Counseling and Mentoring Center
Learning Applicable Relationship Tools

This manual is based in over 22 years experience in professional counseling.

kingdomwellnesscenter@gmail.com

Kingdomshifters.com

KSWU.NET

Connect with Taquetta via Facebook or YouTube

Copyright 2024 – Kingdom Wellness Counseling & Mentor Center. All rights reserved.

Images are either copyright free, public domain images or used with permission of the graphic artist.

This book is protected by the copyright laws of the United States of America. This book may not be reprinted for commercial gain or profit. The use of occasional page copying for personal or group study is permitted and encouraged. Permission will be granted with written request.

TABLE OF CONTENTS

VISION STATEMENT

Kingdom Wellness offers a revolutionary theory of bridging mental and physical health with biblical truths, faith-based counseling, deliverance and healing principles. This is a holistic ideology of the total person – body, soul (mind, will, emotions), and spirit becoming one.

Kingdom Wellness

Mental & Physical Health

Spiritual Well-Being

"Psychological theories are valuable for guiding practice in education, mental health, business, and other domains. They provide answers to intrinsically interesting questions concerning many kinds of thinking including perception, emotion, learning, and problem-solving."[i]

TAQUETTA BAKER, FOUNDER

As an adopted child, Taquetta knows the lifelong journey of appreciating both spiritual and natural relationships and encounters. She understands being strengthened by the pain that life can bring while embracing the joy of unexpected connections. Taquetta has transformed her experiences to establish a legacy of pioneering and fearlessly leading others.

Taquetta Baker is the founder of Kingdom Shifters Ministries (KSM), Kingdom Shifters Empowerment Church, and Kingdom Wellness Counseling and Mentoring Center. She has authored over 50 books and two prayer CD's. Taquetta has a Doctorate in Ministry, a Master's Degree in Community Counseling with an emphasis on Marriage, Children and Family Counseling, a Bachelor's Degree in Psychology and Associates Degree in Business Administration. Taquetta has a Therapon Belief Therapist Certification from the Therapon Institute, which provides faith-based counseling and ministry training. She is a certified Leadership & Executive Life Coach and has written her own Kingdom Wellness Counseling & Life Coaching theory and curriculum.

Taquetta serves in the mental health field as a Behavioral Consultant. She enjoys working with individuals and families who experience a broad range of psychological, emotional, social, relational, and spiritual challenges. Her outreach demonstrates cultural agility across a spectrum of ages, ethnicities, and socio-economic backgrounds. She is committed to empowering others with launching ministries, businesses, and books. She provides mentoring, counseling and vision launching through her Kingdom Wellness Counseling and Mentoring Center. With over 22 years of faith-based and professional counseling experience, her reputation is one who transforms lives and families through balancing biblical principles with applicable tools and strategies.

Taquetta serves on the Board of Directors for New Day Community Ministries, Inc. and is a graduate of the Eagles Dance Institute under Dr. Pamela Hardy with a license in liturgical dance. Before pioneering her own ministry, Taquetta was a dedicated member of Christ Temple Global Ministries for 14 years. She served pioneered Shekinah Expressions dance ministry and served in the role of prophet, teacher, presbytery board member, and overseer of the Altar Workers Ministry. Taquetta receives mentoring and ministry covering from Bishop Jackie Green, Founder of JGM-National Prayer Life Institute (Phoenix, AZ), and was ordained as an Apostle on June 7, 2014.

The Bible is full of stories that are centered around digging or receiving from wells which represent stability and deep places of renewal. Taquetta flows through the spiritual wells of warfare, worship, counseling and deliverance. Taquetta's mantle is an apostolic directive of judging and establishing God's kingdom in people, ministries, communities, and regions. Taquetta travels in foreign missions and throughout the United States. She has mentored and established dance teams, altar workers, counseling programs, and deliverance and prophetic ministries. Taquetta ministers in the areas of fine arts, systems of prayer, fivefold ministry, deliverance, healing, miracles, atmospheric worship, and counseling. Her mission is to empower and train others to identify and embrace their destiny.

Shift!

LIVING AS AN ACCEPTABLE SACRIFICE

I highly recommend purchasing a copy of my manual "*Sustaining The Vision Workbook*." The manual is designed to equip the vision carrier with understanding their destiny and calling and writing their vision, while acquiring Godly revelation on how to pray, release, plow, and sustain in the destiny and calling of God on his or her life. It will assist the vision carrier in learning how to govern the vision as a pure visionary, and how to lead in excellence and SHIFT those who are called to help bring the vision to pass.

Romans 12:1-2 *I beseech you therefore, brethren, by the mercies of God, that ye present your bodies a living sacrifice, holy, acceptable unto God, which is your reasonable service. And be not conformed to this world: but be ye transformed by the renewing of your mind, that ye may prove what is that good, and acceptable, and perfect, will of God.*

<u>*Beseech* is *Parakeo*</u> in the Greek and means:
1. to call near, i.e. invite, invoke (by imploration, hortation (tending or aiming to exhort) or consolation)
2. beseech, call for, (be of good) comfort, desire, (give) exhort(-ation)
3. intreat, pray. to call to one's side, call for, summon, to address
4. speak to (call to, call upon), which may be done in the way of exhortation, entreaty, comfort, instruction, etc.
5. to admonish, exhort, to beg, entreat, beseech, to strive to appease by entreaty
6. to console, to encourage and strengthen by consolation, to comfort, to receive consolation, be comforted
7. to encourage, strengthen, exhorting and comforting and encouragingto instruct, teach

<u>*Mercies* is oiktirmos</u> in Greek and means:
1. pity: — mercy, compassion, pity

2. bowels in which compassion resides, a heart of compassion
3. emotions, longings, manifestations of pity

Apostle Paul was experiencing how God longs with compassion for the people he was shepherding to be who God had created them to be. This mercy was being experienced through the bowels of godly compassion.

- ✓ When you keep being chased down with the same prophecy or word concerning who you are, what God wants you to do, how God wants to use you.

- ✓ When you keep having the same dreams or visions or similar dreams and visions of you doing certain things.

- ✓ When God keeps unctioning you to go forth and do and be a particular thing.

- ✓ When God keeps showing and telling you that you are equipped or that he will equip you to do a particular thing.

You are experiencing the mercies - the compassions of God where he is beseeching you to SHIFT you to embody who he has called you to be.

Let's just ponder this truth for a moment.

So many people have not sacrificed themselves so they cannot and have not positioned themselves to hear God for their calling.

They are not dead to Christ to know what is in them that pleases him.

They are still fashioned by what pleases them, others, or the world - what they want to achieve and accomplish in life.

They are drawn to the identity of the world:

- What the world seems appropriate, acceptable, successful

- What others can handle about them or desire from them rather than to the true identity of God on the inside of them.

They - you - us – we - have not given up our vision of purpose and destiny where we really hear God for his original intent and purpose for our lives.

Growing up, my life's plan was to be married, have children, obtain a master's degree, have a residential facility for girls - all by age 30. As I went through my college years, this was my pursuit. Even at age 24 when I truly gave my life to God this was still the vision I saw clearly in my head. By age 27, the only thing I had accomplished was my master's degree. The more I submitted my life to God, the more my life began to take a different path. I learned later that it was the path of destiny - the path that was pleasing to God.

I did not understand that initially. But my heart burned to please God, yet my actions dreaded the sacrifice. I had to give up everything to be what God wanted, to do what God wanted, to live where God wanted, to fashion into what God wanted, to say what God wanted, to live how God wanted.

No one around me said this is destiny, this is your purpose, this is your calling. No one around me said you are just embodying - beseeching - becoming what pleases God. I wish someone would have told me that dying to self and only doing and being what my father God says was what destiny was - that this dimension of living for God is what it truly meant to *present your body a living sacrifice, holy, acceptable unto God, which is your reasonable service* - reasonable meaning - it is practicable, sensible; appropriate, suitable, fitting, proper, well advised.

But no one said that and as I look back on it, no one around me knew to tell me that.

MY GOD!

Most people poured into me because of my relentless pursuit, not because of the understanding of this passage of scripture or that becoming what God wanted was what salvation was.

Let's just ponder this truth for a moment.

> **SALVATION IS WILLINGLY BECOMING GOD IDENTITY AND EMBRACING THE LOVE, JOY, AND FULFILLMENT OF GOD IS ON THE INSIDE OF YOU!**

I would complain about how I was misunderstood, did not have any friends, did not fit in.

In the world I was the life of the party, I was well liked, known, and regarded for my risk-taking approach to life, thrill-seeking fun-loving personality, quick wit, intelligence and successes. When I began to beseech God, the likeness of him caused people to be repelled by me. Mainly church people who claimed they lived for God and also by people who felt judged by the character and nature of God that was overtaking me.

Though I would sacrifice myself, I did not know this is what I was doing.

I did not know this is what I needed to do.

I hated doing it even though I was driven to please God.

It was not until my late 30s that I understood this was destiny and my joy and fulfillment resided in embracing it with love and adoration unto God. By then I had spent years doing and being who God said, without enjoying and honoring who I was and getting to do what I was purposed to be.

Let's just ponder this truth for a moment.

Calling – Calling is what you are anointed or appointed to do in the earth.

Purpose – Our calling entails our purpose. We were all born with a specific purpose. Our calling allows us to have kingdom impact so we can impart our God identity into the earth. What impact does your calling have on your family, people, lands, communities, regions, and spheres of influence? That is your purpose.

Destiny – Destiny is where we are going in life. Destiny is a progressive journey with God.

> *Strategy* is the goals, behavioral steps, revelations, wisdom, knowledge, accountabilities, supports, partners, provision, a person needs to bring their calling, purpose, or vision to pass - Jer. 29:11, Pro. 16:3, Jam. 1:5, Pro. 3:5-6.

> *Anointing Wells* is how God uses a person in their destiny calling and purpose. No matter what a person is doing you can see this anointing - this yoke breaking well flowing through them. Anointing is also the oil that breaks the yoke as a person operates in their gifts and calling - Isa. 10:27, 1Joh. 2:27, Isa. 61, Luk. 4:18, Lev. 8:12, Mar. 6:13

We all have destiny moments of success, but destiny is a lifestyle journey with the Lord.

- ✓ Your life has to be submitted to God to know, embody, and walk in your calling,

- ✓ You have to want to be what and who God has called you to be.

- ✓ You have to want to please him with your life and deeds.

- ✓ You have to hear him for who you are and how it pleases him and endeavor to do what he says.

So many do not SHIFT into their calling because they have not presented their bodies a living sacrifice.

The Greek word *sacrifice* in *Romans 12* actually means **victim**.

Let's just ponder this truth for a moment.

Dictionary.com defines *victim* as:
1. a person harmed, injured, or killed as a result of a crime, accident, or other event or action
2. a person who is tricked or duped (this is actually how I feel about my destiny - that I was tricked into it)
3. a living creature killed as a religious sacrifice, offerings, a scapegoat
4. fall victim to - be hurt, killed, damaged, or destroyed by

5. sufferer, injured party, casualty, injured person, wounded person; dead person, fatality, loss; loser
6. dupe, easy target, easy prey, fair game, sitting target, everybody's fool, stooge, gull, fool, target, prey, quarry, object, subject, recipient, focus; sitting duck, sucker, fall guy, pushover, soft touch, easy touch, chump

When you become a living sacrifice, you become clay in the potter's hands. You do not dictate to him who you become. You allow him to mold and shape you into who he has created and called you to be.

Isaiah 64:8 But now, O LORD, thou art our father; we are the clay, and thou our potter; and we all are the work of thy hand.

When God is molding and shaping us, he is recreating us to be holy and acceptable according to his original purpose and intent for our lives. **The Amplified Bible** *causes this a rational act of worship.*

The Amplified Bible *Therefore I urge you, brothers and sisters, by the mercies of God, to present your bodies [dedicating all of yourselves, set apart] as a living sacrifice, holy and well-pleasing to God, which is your rational (logical, intelligent) act of worship.*

Our job is not to conform to this world so we can be transformed into purpose, holiness, a well pleasing - logical - act of worship - what pleases God.

Conformed is *syschēmatizō* in the Greek and means:
1. to fashion alike, i.e. conform to the same pattern (figuratively)
2. conform to, fashion self-according to
3. to conform oneself (i.e. one's mind and character) to another's pattern, (fashion oneself according to)

In order to hear God about your calling, trust what he is saying, align with it, walk in it, you have to first pursue him and truly live for him. And then you have to sacrifice yourself to him and be willing to come out of anything that would fashion you in your own desired image, the world's image, Satan's image.

Sacrificing will not feel good because it is a literal death such that you live in Christ Jesus.

Galatians 2:20 I have been crucified with Christ; it is no longer I who live, but Christ lives in me; and the life which I now live in the flesh I live by faith in the Son of God, who loved me and gave Himself for me.

You become a victim that allows God to do in and with you what he will.

John 4:34 *Jesus saith unto them, My meat is to do the will of him that sent me, and to finish his work.*

John 5:19-20 *Then answered Jesus and said unto them, Verily, verily, I say unto you, The Son can do nothing of himself, but what he seeth the Father do: for what things soever he doeth, these also doeth the Son likewise. For the Father loveth the Son, and sheweth him all things that himself doeth: and he will shew him greater works than these, that ye may marvel.*

John 6:38 *For I came down from heaven, not to do mine own will, but the will of him that sent me.*

Matthew 7:21-27 *Not every one that saith unto me, Lord, Lord, shall enter into the kingdom of heaven; but he that doeth the will of my Father which is in heaven. Many will say to me in that day, Lord, Lord, have we not prophesied in thy name? and in thy name have cast out devils? and in thy name done many wonderful works? And then will I profess unto them, I never knew you: depart from me, ye that work iniquity.*

Therefore whosoever heareth these sayings of mine, and doeth them, I will liken him unto a wise man, which built his house upon a rock: And the rain descended, and the floods came, and the winds blew, and beat upon that house; and it fell not: for it was founded upon a rock. And every one that heareth these sayings of mine, and doeth them not, shall be likened unto a foolish man, which built his house upon the sand: And the rain descended, and the floods came, and the winds blew, and beat upon that house; and it fell: and great was the fall of it.

Ephesians 4:13 *Till we all come in the unity of the faith, and of the knowledge of the Son of God, unto a perfect man, unto the measure of the stature of the fullness of Christ.*

In order to allow God to fashion you, you have to hunger to be like him and to please him. It has to burn in you while being manna you long to feast off of. It has to be a pursuit with the cost of everything for salvation is free, but destiny will cost you everything.

The scripture lets us know that this level of conformity unto God requires a renewing of the mind. A renewing of the mind is essential to being a victim in the hands of God, and allowing him to mold, shape, and grounded you in his will, plan, and truth of your purpose, calling and destiny.

A renewing of the mind is when we reject our thoughts and ways and seek to learn, embody, live, and continuously set our thoughts on what is of God and what pleases God.

Transformation in the Greek is _metamorphoō_ and means:

1. to transform (literally or figuratively, "metamorphose")
2. change, transfigure, transform
3. to change into another form, to transform, to transfigure
4. Christ appearance was changed and was resplendent with divine brightness on the mount of transfiguration

When we go through a metamorphosis, we completely SHIFT into someone totally different than who we were. Therefore, our minds become like God's rather than like the worlds. Our ideals, perceptions, and processings are no longer like the world.

- We think and reason like God.

- We recognize, discern, comprehend and envision like God.

- We evolve in the image and likeness of God.

- We in turn behave in the character and nature of God.

- We are filled with the vision of God and envision to be and do what he shows and demonstrated to us.

- We crave and eat his likeness and feast only on what pleasures of his identity.

Isaiah 55:8-13 The Amplified Bible _For My thoughts are not your thoughts, Nor are your ways My ways," declares the LORD. "For as the heavens are higher than the earth, So are My ways higher than your ways And My thoughts higher than your thoughts._

"For as the rain and snow come down from heaven, And do not return there without watering the earth, Making it bear and sprout, And providing seed to the sower and bread to the eater, So will My word be which goes out of My mouth; It will not return to Me void (useless, without result), Without accomplishing what I desire, And without succeeding in the matter for which I sent it. "For you will go out [from exile] with joy And be led forth [by the LORD Himself] with peace;

The mountains and the hills will break forth into shouts of joy before you, And all the trees of the field will clap their hands. "Instead of the thorn bush the cypress tree will grow, And instead of the nettle the myrtle tree will grow; And it will be a memorial to the LORD, For an everlasting sign [of His mercy] which will not be cut off."

Though God's ways and thoughts are above ours, the Bible does not say we cannot achieve them. Continual abiding, evolving, maturing, and SHIFTING higher in Christ likeness enables us to capture and achieve his ways and thoughts.

The Amplified Bible *And do not be conformed to this world [any longer with its superficial values and customs], but be transformed and progressively changed [as you mature spiritually] by the renewing of your mind [focusing on godly values and ethical attitudes], so that you may prove [for yourselves] what the will of God is, that which is good and acceptable and perfect [in His plan and purpose for you].*

As you become acceptable to God, you endeavor to glorify him through who he has molded and shaped you to be.

In order to meet the standards of a living sacrifice, what you do has to be:

- Good - of good constitution or nature, useful, salutary, pleasant, agreeable, joyful, happy, excellent, distinguishedupright, honorable

- Acceptable - well pleasing
- Perfect - abor, growth, mental and moral character, etc.); completeness; of full age, man, perfect, brought to its end, finishedwanting nothing necessary to completeness

- His will - purpose, decree, volition or (passively) inclination; desire, pleasure, will, choice, what he wishes or has determined shall be done, of what God wishes to be done by us; his commands, precepts

This demonstrates:

- The that you are not fashioned by your own image, the word's conformity or that of demons.

- You have his mind about who you are and what you are purposed to do.

- Clarity in your calling.

- A forsaking of all else, while using your gifts, talents, and life's purpose *proving what is that good, and acceptable, and perfect, will of God.*

This means your purpose, calling, and identity, is used:

- Where he desires

- How he desires

- For who he desires

- When he desires

You do not sing for the world and act like it glorified God.

You do not put a godly twist on a vision or endeavor you know is fashioned by the world or demons and call it acceptable unto God.

You do not engage in sinful or shrewd business practices and because it causes you to prosper, you claim it is the blessings of God.

You cannot walk in a measure of obedience to what he is saying you are to be and claim it of God.

You cannot continue to reject the mercy drawings of God and claim you cannot hear or do not know your calling.

You cannot lack relationship with God then contend it is his fault or your pastor's fault that you do not know your calling.

You cannot continue to be shaped in inadequacy and insecurity while rejecting the truth of your calling. Often, we are trying to acquire boldness, confidence, and authority first. However, accepting the truth of your calling and allowing God to mold and shape you in it, is what SHIFTS you into boldness, confidence, and authority to walk in it. Moreover, as you become a sacrifice in his hands, he gives you a life's vision plan that entails the biblical standards you need to sustain in the destiny calling on your life.

When we are not conformed to the fashions and identity God regarding our calling, purpose, and destiny, can lend to strange fire and idolatry.

Strange fire is when we offer up a sacrifice that is foreign and or contrary to his, word, will, plans, character, nature.

Idolatry is when we offer up sacrifices to other gods - this committing adultery against God.

This is the reason you must allow God to tell and guide you in destiny.

This is also the reason you must check what you do and make sure it is HOLY, acceptable, and pleasing to God.

Be clay in his hands so he can potter you in his design.

SHIFT RIGHT NOW! SHIFT!

From my manual, *"Healing The Wounded Leader."*

It is important to be clear and pure in your motives when pursuing your destiny.

- *Proverbs 21:2 Every way of a man [is] right in his own eyes: but the LORD pondereth the hearts.*

- *The Message Bible We justify our actions by appearances; God examines our motives.*

- *Matthew 6:1 Take heed that ye do not your alms before men, to be seen of them: otherwise ye have no reward of your Father which is in heaven.*

- *Proverbs 30:12 There is a generation that are pure in their own eyes, and yet is not washed from their filthiness.*

When our motives are impure:

- We will think God is pleased with things we do that really do not possess his character or nature (*Matthew 7:23 And then will I profess unto them, I never knew you: depart from me, ye that work iniquity*).

- We will call right wrong and wrong right (*Isaiah 50:20 The Living Bible They say that what is right is wrong and what is wrong is right; that black is white and white is black; bitter is sweet and sweet is bitter*).

- We will think we are Godly but be full of filth and debauchery (*Ephesians 5:10-11 Determine which things please the Lord. Have nothing to do with the useless works that darkness produces. Instead, expose them for what they are*).

- We will be guided by what we see (*1John 2:16 For everything in the world--the lust of the flesh, the lust of the eyes, and the pride of life--comes not from the Father but from the world*).

- Seek to please people and gain the applause of people instead of God *(Galatians 1:10 For do I now persuade men, or God? or do I seek to please men? for if I yet pleased men, I should not be the servant of Christ).*

As God makes you a living sacrifice, represent him well. Represent him with excellent. **SHINE FOR HIM.**

- Do not remain in a cave God did not put you in.

- Do not stay too long on the backside of the dessert when God has called you forth to lead and to rule.

- Do not hide the truth of his power and authority in you.

- Do not water or dummy yourself down.

- Do not defend or make excuses regarding the excellency, abilities, capabilities, potential, capacity, successes that you embody.

- Do not worry about or conform to what people and the world can handle about you.

- Do not let the insecurities, jealousies, and envies of people cause you to diminish or cower in the light and glory of who God is in you.

- Do not reject the opportunities to shine for Jesus. When the door opens - the platform presents itself - step into the destiny moment and SHINE for Jesus.

- Do not let people and demons tell you that you are doing too much. Your life can never cease in getting and giving God glory.

Be fearfully and wonderfully made as you demonstrate the excellency and power of God that is on the inside of you.

Psalm 139:14 I will praise thee; for I am fearfully and wonderfully made: marvellous are thy works; and that my soul knoweth right well.

2Corinthians 4:4-7 In whom the god of this world hath blinded the minds of them which believe not, lest the light of the glorious gospel of Christ, who is the image of God, should shine unto them. For we preach not ourselves, but Christ Jesus the Lord; and ourselves your servants for Jesus' sake. For God, who commanded the light to shine out of darkness, hath shined in our hearts, to give the light of the knowledge of the glory of God in the face of Jesus Christ. But we have this treasure in earthen vessels, that the excellency of the power may be of God, and not of us.

<u>Excellency is *hyperbolē* in Greek and means:</u>
1. a throwing beyond others, i.e. (figuratively) supereminence; pre- eminently
2. abundance, (far more) exceeding, excellency, more excellent, beyond (out of) measure, beyond all measure

Daniel 5:12 *Forasmuch as an excellent spirit, and knowledge, and understanding, interpreting of dreams, and shewing of hard sentences, and dissolving of doubts, were found in the same Daniel, whom the king named Belteshazzar: now let Daniel be called, and he will shew the interpretation.*

Daniel 6:3 *This Daniel was preferred above the presidents and princes, because an excellent spirit was in him; and the king thought to set him over the whole realm.*

<u>Excellent is *yatiyr* in the Hebrew and means:</u>
1. preeminent; as an adverb, very
2. exceeding, exceedingly, excellent, extraordinary
3. pre-eminent (superior, distinguished, towering),
4. surpassing, extreme

<u>Dictionary.com defines *excellent* as:</u>
1. possessing outstanding quality or superior merit
2. remarkably good
3. Archaic. extraordinary; superior

Achieving excellency is not through your strength but the power of the Holy Spirit on the inside of you. Your abiding covenant relationship with God shapes you into his excellency so your God likeness can glorify him.

BE YOU!
BE GREAT!

BE & OPERATE IN AN EXCELLENT SPIRIT!

GIVE HIM GLORY!

SHINE FOR JESUS!

SHIFT RIGHT NOW!

Shifting Activation: (Please know that you may have to study this entire book before answering these questions strategically and clearly. It would also be beneficial to answer the questions now then once you study this book, answer them again. This will give you greater detailed revelation on understanding your calling and purpose sufficiently and vastly).

1. Journal on your life as it is now. Share where you are in life, where you are in God, your relationship with God, and anything else he reveals to you.

2. Journal in detail any promises and prophecies God has spoken over your life. Highlight repeated prophecies and promises.

3. Seek God and journal in detail what he says your purpose is, calling is, destiny is.

4. Journal what your anointing wells are as you consider how God uses you in your destiny and calling.

5. Journal your understanding of what it means to be a living sacrifice according to this teaching.

6. Seek God for truth as to whether you have become a living sacrifice according to this teaching. Journal what he says.

7. Journal what ways you need to be renewed in your mind, to forsake the world, and people to become a living sacrifice.

8. Journal the challenges and struggles you have with being renewed in your mind and resisting the conformity of the world.

9. Journal in detail what God says is a reasonable service of being sold out to him. Journal what you need to sacrifice to be just that. Ask him for a love for what you have to sacrifice to love and be fulfilled by the journey of your calling.

10. Seek God and journal what he deems is holy, acceptable, perfect, his will regarding your destiny and calling.

11. Ask him to show you him doing it and you doing it for him. Endeavor to live doing what your father God shows you as a daily lifestyle. Shine for him and let your life give him glory.

CALLINGS & ANOINTING WELLS

Revelation From Taquetta Baker's Kingdom Wellness Spiritual Coaching Manual Copyright January 2024

Calling – Calling is what you are anointed or appointed to do in the earth.

Purpose – Our calling entails our purpose. We were all born with a specific purpose. Our calling allows us to have kingdom impact so we can impart our God identity into the earth. What impact does your calling have on your family, people, lands, communities, regions, and spheres of influence? That is your purpose.

Destiny – Destiny is where we are going in life. Destiny is a progressive journey with God. We all have destiny moments of success, but destiny is a lifestyle journey with the Lord.

Genesis 1:26-28 And God said, Let us make man in our image, after our likeness: and let them have dominion over the fish of the sea, and over the fowl of the air, and over the cattle, and over all the earth, and over every creeping thing that creepeth upon the earth. So God created man in his own image, in the image of God created he him; male and female created he them. And God blessed them, and God said unto them, Be fruitful, and multiply, and replenish the earth, and subdue it: and have dominion over the fish of the sea, and over the fowl of the air, and over every living thing that moveth upon the earth.

Proverbs 19:21 *Many plans are in a man's mind, but it is the Lord's purpose for him that will stand.*

Psalm 119:105 *Your word is a lamp to my feet, and a light to my path.*

Natural & Learned Talents - Talents are skills and abilities that you do well. All talents are not listed in the bible, but are a grace, uniqueness, and ability to do something with supernatural uniqueness and ability that others may or may not have, and even if they do have it, it is not a prototype of you or your talent. An example of talents would be playing the piano, a musical instrument, singing, being a great athlete, being a genius, skilled at math, etc. If you do it well and it comes naturally to you, it is probably a talent that God supernaturally gifted you with.

Skill & Expertise - Expertise falls under natural talents. Expertise entails an expert skill or knowledge, expertness, field of study, passion, or compassion; or know-how regarding a topic, population of people, region, arena, or sphere of influence. This expertise can be learned through personal experience, watching and assisting others who have experienced it, educational learning, training and equipping, self-teaching and training. The peson can also have a natural knack for learning on different subjects, thus becoming an expert. Because of a person's spiritual gifts, they will see a need and become an expert by fulfilling that need. Please understand that God blesses talents and expertise even as he blesses spiritual gifts. He will also fill us with skill and abilities.

Exodus 31:6 *And behold, I Myself have appointed with him Oholiab, the son of Ahisamach, of the tribe of Dan; and in the hearts of all who are skillful I have put skill, that they may make all that I have commanded you:*

Exodus 35:35 *He has filled them with skill to perform every work of an engraver and of a designer and of an embroiderer, in blue and in purple and in scarlet material, and in fine linen, and of a weaver, as performers of every work and makers of designs.*

Spiritual Gifts - Spiritual gifts are in the bible. They are gifts empowered in us through God's Holy Spirit. They are giftings that God has given for the purposes of saving the lost, bringing deliverance and healing to people, lands, and regions, and establishing God's kingdom in the earth. Though you are born with some gifts, you can ask Holy Spirit for gifts and he can awaken them in you as he desires. Studying the word and pursuing the gifts can always activate and mature them in you.

Romans 12:6-8 Having then gifts differing according to the grace that is given to us, whether prophecy, let us prophesy according to the proportion of faith; Or ministry, let us wait on our ministering: or he that teacheth, on teaching; Or he that exhorteth, on exhortation: he that giveth, let him do it with simplicity; he that ruleth, with diligence; he that sheweth mercy, with cheerfulness.

1Corinthians 12:8-10 For to one is given by the Spirit the word of wisdom; to another the word of knowledge by the same Spirit; To another faith by the same Spirit; to another the gifts of healing by the same Spirit; To another the working of miracles; to another prophecy; to another discerning of spirits; to another divers kinds of tongues; to another the interpretation of tongues:

1Corinthians 12:28-31 And God hath set some in the church, first apostles, secondarily prophets, thirdly teachers, after that miracles, then gifts of healings, helps, governments, diversities of tongues. Are all apostles? are all prophets? are all teachers? are all workers of miracles? Have all the gifts of healing? do all speak with tongues? do all interpret? But covet earnestly the best gifts: and yet shew I unto you a more excellent way.

Gifts and talents operate through the wells of our calling. Many people operate in their gifts and talents but lack understanding in their calling so they are erred or fail to walk in their divine purpose. If you are a leader, it is important for you to know your calling and the spiritual gifts and natural talents you operate in. It is equally important to know the reason a person is called to release the vision or ministry endeavor you are assisting them with, how it impacts the earth, and how to awaken their gifts and talents so they flourish in their calling through that vision.

Kingdom Vision - Vision is the journey and plans our lives will take to operate in our calling and achieve destiny.

Isaiah 58:8-13 New International Bible For my thoughts are not your thoughts, neither are your ways my ways," declares the LORD. "As the heavens are higher than the earth, so are my ways higher than your ways and my thoughts than your thoughts. As the rain and the snow come down from heaven, and do not return to it without watering the earth and making it bud and flourish, so that it yields seed for the sower and bread for the eater, so is my word that goes out from my mouth: It will not return to me empty, but will accomplish what I desire and achieve the purpose for which I sent it. You will go out in joy and be led forth in peace; the mountains and hills will burst into song before you, and all the trees of the field will clap their hands. Instead of the thornbush will grow the juniper, and instead of briers the myrtle will grow. This will be for the LORD's renown, for an everlasting sign, that will endure forever.

Luke 1:37 For no Word from God will ever fail.

Psalm 77:14 You are the God Who performs miracles; You display Your power among the peoples.

Psalm 104:30-31 The Amplified Bible When You send forth Your Spirit and give them breath, they are created, and You replenish the face of the ground. May the glory of the Lord endure forever; may the Lord rejoice in His works.

Luke 18:27 Jesus replied, "What is impossible with man is possible with God."

Jeremiah 32:27 I am the Lord, the God of all mankind. Is anything too hard for Me?

Psalm 139:11 If I say, "Surely the darkness will hide me and the light [will] become night around me," even the darkness will not be dark to You; the night will shine like the day, for darkness is as light to You.

Matthew 17:20 He replied, "Because You have so little faith. Truly I tell you, if you have faith as small as a mustard seed, you can say to this mountain, 'Move from here to there,' and it will move. Nothing will be impossible for you.

1Corinthians 9:24 Do you not know that in a race all the runners run, but only one receives the prize? So run that you may obtain it.

Hebrews 12:10-12 For they verily for a few days chastened us after their own pleasure; but he for our profit, that we might be partakers of his holiness. Now no chastening for the present seemeth to be joyous, but grievous: nevertheless afterward it yieldeth the peaceable fruit of righteousness unto them which are exercised thereby. Wherefore lift up the hands which hang down, and the feeble knees; And make straight paths for your feet, lest that which is lame be turned out of the way; but let it rather be healed.

Ecclesiastes 9:10 *Whatever your hand finds to do, do it with your might, for there is no work or thought or knowledge or wisdom in Sheol, to which you are going.*

Colossians 3:23 *Whatever you do, work heartily, as for the Lord and not for men.*

2Timothy 3:16-17 **The Amplified Bible** *Every Scripture is God-breathed (given by His inspiration) and profitable for instruction, for reproof and conviction of sin, for correction of error and discipline in obedience, [and] for training in righteousness (in holy living, in conformity to God's will in thought, purpose, and action), So that the man of God may be complete and proficient, well fitted and thoroughly equipped for every good work.*

Philippians 3:12-14 *Not that I have already obtained this or am already perfect, but I press on to make it my own, because Christ Jesus has made me his own. Brothers, I do not consider that I have made it my own. But one thing I do: forgetting what lies behind and straining forward to what lies ahead, I press on toward the goal for the prize of the upward call of God in Christ Jesus.*

Habakkuk 2:1-4 *I will stand upon my watch, and set me upon the tower, and will watch to see what he will say unto me, and what I shall answer when I am reproved. And the Lord answered me, and said, Write the vision, and make it plain upon tables, that he may run that readeth it.*

For the vision is yet for an appointed time, but at the end it shall speak, and not lie: though it tarry, wait for it; because it will surely come, it will not tarry. Behold, his soul which is lifted up is not upright in him: but the just shall live by his faith.

Habakkuk took a stand and established himself upon the tower, so he could watch for what God was saying and desiring for him, the call of God for his life, and those he was leading.

A tower is a high place, a mound, fortress, siege, entrenchment, and enclosure.

It is generally upon a horizon which yields what is to come - or yield the beginnings and future of things. It reveals that which is afar off.

Because the tower is upon the horizon, it also allows the watchman:

- To see who is coming and going
- See the enemy afar off
- Provides the watchman time to signal and warn that the enemy is approaching or what is occurring in the distance

Habakkuk SHIFTED himself to a heightened dimension in God, while enclosing himself in this realm where he could see past his circumstances into the truth and will of God. This was a time of consecration for he took a time of stillness before the Lord, "I will stand upon my watch, and set me upon the tower, and will watch to see what he will say."

Kingdom Activation:

1. Spend time jounaling what you learned from this chapter and how it impacts your life.

2. Spend time journaling what makes you you, what makes you unique.

3. Spend time journaling the good and the negative life patterns you have had and how they have shaped your:

- Personality (Character, nature, how you engage, interact, impress, and impact others; how they engage, interact, impress and impact you)

- Identity (Who you are and who God is in you; what makes you unique; what makes you your whole self – an entire person that reveals to truth, fruit, and salvation of God)

- Mindset (How you think, perceive; what you consider; your understanding of yourself, life and others; your beliefs, morals, values, and ideologies)

- Emotions (How you feel about yourself, others, life itself, your present and future state, abilities, and successes. Your ability to feel, process how you feel, be balanced in your feelings, handle life experiences in an emotionally stable manner)

- Heart (What you treasure, value, hold in high esteem – high regard; what matters most to you in life)
- Soul (Your mental and emotional wellness; life stability, posture with challenging and traumatic life events; personal and generational bondages, blessings)

- Life (Your ability to live present and futuristic in life; your ability to leave the past behind yet learn from your experiences, especially your mistakes; your life opportunities, successive, motives, intents, purposes, standards)

- Relationships (Your relationship with God; your relationship with people; your desire and pursuit of relationships; how you operate in relationships; your ability to have good relationships; be loyal, faithful, loving, accountable, and stable in relationships; your ability to identify who should and should not be in your life; your ability to have godly covenant relationships)

4. Spend time using the revelation below to seek God for clarity of your destiny and purpose. Be mindful of the questions in the first chapter.

5. Journal what you learned and how it applies to your life.

6. Jounal what your gifts, talents, calling, purpose, anointing wells, and vision is in life is.

7. Spend time seeking and journaling with God for kingdom vision concerning who you are and how your purpose, calling, and destiny impact the kingdom of God and the world at large. Be specific regarding:

   - The people you are called to.
   - The regions, communities, and environments you are called to.
   - The spheres of influence you are called to.
   - How your personality and unique God identity impact these people, regions, communities, environments, and spheres of influence.

If you have experienced a lot of hardship and trauma in your life, I highly recommend purchasing my *Destiny Recoding MP3 and PDF*. It will help you heal in the areas of trauma while processing you to recoding your destiny to GOD's original intent and purpose for your life. It is available at kingdomshiftingbooks.com and on teachable.com.

GIFTINGS & OFFICES

Revelation From Taquetta Baker's Kingdom Wellness Spiritual Coaching Manual Copyright January 2024.

Spiritual Gifts

Spiritual gifts are in the bible. They are gifts empowered in us through God's Holy Spirit. They are giftings that God has given for the purposes of saving the lost, bringing deliverance and healing to people, lands, and regions, and establishing God's kingdom in the earth. Though you are born with some gifts, you can ask Holy Spirit for gifts, and he can awaken them in you as he desires. Studying the word and pursuing the gifts can always activate and mature them in you.

Spiritual Gifts In The Bible:

Romans 12:6–8	1Corinthians 12:8–10	1Corinthians 12:28
• Prophecy	• Word of wisdom	• Apostle
• Serving	• Word of knowledge	• Prophet
• Teaching	• Faith	• Teacher
• Exhortation	• Gifts of healings	• Miracles
• Giving	• Miracles	• Kinds of healings
• Leadership	• Prophecy	• Helps
• Mercy	• Distinguishing between spirits	• Administration

	• Tongues	• Tongues
	• Interpretation of tongues	

Romans 12:6-8 *Having then gifts differing according to the grace that is given to us, whether prophecy, let us prophesy according to the proportion of faith; Or ministry, let us wait on our ministering: or he that teacheth, on teaching; Or he that exhorteth, on exhortation: he that giveth, let him do it with simplicity; he that ruleth, with diligence; he that sheweth mercy, with cheerfulness.*

1Corinthians 12:8-10 *For to one is given by the Spirit the word of wisdom; to another the word of knowledge by the same Spirit; To another faith by the same Spirit; to another the gifts of healing by the same Spirit; To another the working of miracles; to another prophecy; to another discerning of spirits; to another divers kinds of tongues; to another the interpretation of tongues:*

1Corinthians 12:28-31 *And God hath set some in the church, first apostles, secondarily prophets, thirdly teachers, after that miracles, then gifts of healings, helps, governments, diversities of tongues. Are all apostles? are all prophets? are all teachers? are all workers of miracles? Have all the gifts of healing? do all speak with tongues? do all interpret? But covet earnestly the best gifts: and yet shew I unto you a more excellent way.*

Gifts and talents operate through the wells of our calling. Many people operate in their gifts and talents but lack understanding in their calling, so they are erred or fail to walk in their divine purpose. As a leader, is important for you to know your calling and the spiritual gifts and natural talents you operate in. It is equally important to know the reason a person is called to release the vision or ministry endeavor you are assisting them with, how it impacts the earth, and how to awaken their gifts and talents so they flourish in their calling through that vision.

DEFINING THE BIBLICAL GIFTS

Gift of Helps – People with the gift of helps have the joyful and exuberant ability to work up front and behind the scenes to get things done. They are self-sacrificing, loyal, hard workers, possess a servant's heart, persevering, while being able to shoulder burdens without become overwhelmed or viewing it as an obligation, pressure, or weight. Such persons have a keen attention to detail, can see beyond the current vision or obstacle. They have ability to see what needs to be done without being told what is needed or waiting on someone to do it. They will work their role in a peson's life and vision with excitement and honor.

A person with the gift of helps will need to be very balanced so that they make sure they are not doing things for peson that they should be doing for themselves. Ultimately, unless it is a partnership, the vision and responsibility for the vision belongs to the visionary. Helpers must know their role in the visionary's life and vision and be mindful not to be or do more than what God is requiring. If a helper cross these boundaries, it results in them being the fixer and rescue rather than the one who helps and empowers.

Gift of Exhortation – The gift of exhortation equips a person to encourage, empower, edify, motivate, affirm, convey, breathe life and miracles into people, visions, atmospheres, and regions. A person with this gift operates through the sovereignty of God. They are clear and unwavering about God's character, nature, abilities, capabilities, and they are able to empower people to trust his sovereignty (*Acts 11:23-24, Acts 14:21-22, Acts 15:32, Romans 12:7-8, Romans 14:19 Romans 15:2, John 14:16, 2Timothy 4:2, 1Thessalonians 5:11*).

Gift of Knowledge – *Knowledge* in Greek is **gnósis** meaning *"knowledge, science, doctrine, intelligence, or divine understanding."* It is the knowledge of God offered to advance the gospel through what has been conveyed.

A person with this gift possess the ability to have spiritual facts, information, understanding regarding people, places, lands, spheres, and things. They will receive words of knowledge regarding the person's past and present life and experiences, insight on hidden mysteries regarding that person or in relations to people, interactions, places, directions, transitions, traps, hinderances, opportunities, etc. People with this gift can exemplify knowledge beyond their years, natural understanding, or expertise. They have no means of proving what they know other than by the Holy Spirit and the confirmation of others. When they study information or receive more training and equipping, they receive increased knowledge from the Holy Spirit that further catapults them beyon their educational levels or expertise.

The person brings forth, report, make known, give facts, pass on, convey awareness, have insight, understanding, intelligence via the Holy Spirit. What they share is intended to draw people into trusting God and posturing them in a place of receiving deliverance, healing, prophecy, wisdom, strategy, and instruction to advance their lives and vision through the purpose of God.

Gift of Prophecy - Prophecy in the Greek is ***prophēteia*** and means *"prediction (scriptural or other), a discourse emanating from divine inspiration and declaring the purposes of God, whether by reproving and admonishing the wicked, or comforting the afflicted, or revealing things hidden; esp. by foretelling future events."*

Those with the gift of prophecy possess the ability to edify, comfort, and exhort a peson or body of people. Many people will be testifiersof the goodness of Jesus. They will have many testimonies regarding the successes God has led them and clients to achieve. And they will understand and value the truth of how testifying breeds an atmosphere for breakthrough and miracles.

Revelations 19:9-10 *And he saith unto me, Write, Blessed are they which are called unto the marriage supper of the Lamb. And he saith unto me, These are the true sayings of God. And I fell at his feet to worship him. And he said unto me, See thou do it not: I am thy fellowservant, and of thy brethren that have the testimony of Jesus: worship God: for the testimony of Jesus is the spirit of prophecy.*

People with a prophetic gift will be able to release words of knowledge and revelation regarding a peson's past and present, while also providing foresight into the future. If there is no foresight, it is not prophecy, just the spirit of knowledge and revelation at work. This is fine as person's can use this information to seek God regarding how to proceed in their present and future lives.

If a person is in the office of a prophet, they may judge, rebuke, correct, direct, display the anger of the Lord to a people, region, or nation. They can train, equip, and govern others in the areas of prophecy, their prophetic calling and mantle, marketplace ministry, business, pioneering, entrepreneurship, etc. They also govern regions and spheres as they are holy principalities combating the demonic influences and workings of principalities, powers, and territorial spirits.

Gift of Faith - This gift is different than faith unto salvation (which all believers can embody). The gift of faith involves the supernatural ability to believe and trust God in extenuating circumstances for extraordinary results. People with the gift of faith often manifests incredible miracles. They have faith in who they are and in God's ability to produce miracles into what they are believing God for. The gift of faith is essential to standing steadfast in the wisdom and prophecy that God provides, while operating in one's destiny and calling.

Romans 10:17 *So then faith cometh by hearing, and hearing by the word of God.*

Hebrews 11:6 *But without faith it is impossible to please him: for he that cometh to God must believe that he is, and that he is a rewarder of them that diligently seek him.*

Hebrews 11:1 *Now faith is the substance of things hoped for, the evidence of things not seen.*

Gift of Wisdom - People with this gift have the ability to make wise decisions and to advise others similarly. This wisdom isn't just from trial and error in their own lives but through supernatural understanding from God. Such persons see clearly through confusing circumstances and direct themselves and others toward God's will and direction, while standing in the principles of his biblical word.

Proverbs 1:5 *The wise also will hear and increase in learning, and the person of understanding will acquire skill and attain to sound counsel [so that he may be able to steer his course rightly].*

Proverbs 3:13-18 *Blessed are those who find wisdom, those who gain understanding, for she is more profitable than silver and yields better returns than gold. She is more precious than rubies; nothing you desire can compare with her. Long life is in her right hand; in her left hand are riches and honor. Her ways are pleasant ways, and all her paths are peace. She is a tree of life to those who take hold of her; those who hold her fast will be blessed.*

Proverbs 2:6 *For the Lord gives wisdom; from his mouth come knowledge and understanding.*

Proverbs 4:7 *Wisdom is the principal thing; therefore get wisdom: and with all thy getting get understanding.*

Proverbs 16:16 *How much better is it to get wisdom than gold! and to get understanding rather to be chosen than silver!*

Psalm 111:10 *The fear of the Lord is the beginning of wisdom; all who follow his precepts have good understanding. To him belongs eternal praise.*

2Chronicles 1:10-12 *Give me now wisdom and knowledge, that I may go out and come in before this people: for who can judge this thy people, that is so great? And God said to Solomon, Because this was in thine heart, and thou hast not asked riches, wealth, or honour, nor the life of thine enemies, neither yet hast asked long life; but hast asked wisdom and knowledge for thyself, that thou mayest judge my people, over whom I have made thee king: Wisdom and knowledge is* *granted unto thee; and I will give thee riches, and wealth, and honour, such as none of the kings have had that have been before thee, neither shall there any after thee have the like.*

Luke 21:15 *For I will give you words and wisdom that none of your adversaries will be able to resist or contradict.*

<u>*Wisdom in Hebrew is hâkemâ* and means:</u>
1. wisdom (in a good sense), skilful, wisely, wit.
2. skilful man, wits
3. wisdom skill (in war)
4. wisdom (in administration) shrewdness
5. wisdom, prudence (in religious affairs) (
    Dictionary.com defines prudent as:
    a. wise or judicious in practical affairs, sagacious, discreet or circumspect; sober
    b. careful in providing for the future; provident
    c. the quality of having or showing good powers of judgement
    d. caution with regard to practical matters; discretion
    e. regard for one's own interests, provident care in the management of resources; economy; frugality
6. wisdom (ethical and religious)

King Solomon knew that wisdom was more valuable than riches. He knew that if he had wisdom, he could create riches and make wise decisions in his sustaining in what he built from God. When King Solomon failed to follow the wisdom of God, it impacted his kingdom and his generations. We must value wisdom and want to hear godly wisdom. We must have wisdom and have understanding with how to utilize the wisdom they receive. Wisdom is a skillful administrative warfare tactic that keeps the person's destiny and vision in alignment with God. When wisdom is not honored and utilized, the person and the vision become exposed. They become open doors to people, the world, and demons, infiltrating, altering, hindering, or aborting the progress and work of the person and the vision.

Discerning of Spirits – This gift is also referred to "distinguishing between spirits." People with this gift have the ability to discern whether a situation, person, or event is good or evil, right or wrong, heavenly or demonic. This gift is important because it can help protect the person, their vision, and lead them in the right direction.

Discernment in the Greek language (*diakrisis*) means judicial estimation, discern, disputation. It comes from a word meaning to *separate thoroughly, withdraw, oppose, discriminate, decide, hesitate, contend, make to differ, doubt, judge, be partial, stagger, waver.*

Discernment of spirits provides a person the spiritual ability to see, hear, have a sense that a person, place, thing, situation, or matter, is demons, darkness, or evil.
Discernment gives a person the ability to know that something, somebody, some perception, some ideology, is wrong, evil, ungodly, half true, mixed in good and bad concepts which makes it defiled, unhealthy, or godly.

Most people think that if they have an inkling, intuition, or suspicion about something, they are operating in the gift of discernment. But unless you actually have the Holy Spirit and are guided by the Holy Spirit, you are most likely:

- ✓ Receiving a warning from God to try and keep you safe, but this is his grace, conviction, warning, and love operating, more so than you truly having the gift of discernment.

- ✓ Operating through your human reasoning. Depending on your maturity level, intuitiveness, street smarts, desire and drive to be a good person, desire to make safe and responsible decisions, human reasoning can help you to make right decisions and good moral decisions.

- ✓ People can also open a third eye via witchcraft which enables them to use familiar spirits to receive entail or probe people for information that makes them appear they are spiritually discerning.

The gift of discernment is actually factual and true. The gift of discernment is given by the spirit of God - it is the Holy Spirit working and identifying truth in us and around us. What makes it to feel like questioning or cause us to question is our human nature,

- ✓ Our own human thoughts, feelings, and will
- ✓ Our lack of understanding of what discernment is
- ✓ Our lack of understanding that we have this ability in us as part of our gift and calling.

- ✓ It can also be to a lack of having on the full armor of God, or our flesh, mind, & feelings being exalted above our spirit man. This is the reason the Bible encourages us to live through our spirit, such that we trust what he reveals to us.

> *Romans 8:12-16 Therefore, brethren, we are debtors, not to the flesh, to live after the flesh. For if ye live after the flesh, ye shall die: but if ye through the Spirit do mortify the deeds of the body, ye shall live. For as many as are led by the Spirit of God, they are the*

sons of God. For ye have not received the spirit of bondage again to fear; but ye have received the Spirit of adoption, whereby we cry, Abba, Father. The Spirit itself beareth witness with our spirit, that we are the children of God: And if children, then heirs; heirs of God, and joint-heirs with Christ; if so be that we suffer with him, that we may be also glorified together.

Galatians 5:16-18 *This I say then, Walk in the Spirit, and ye shall not fulfil the lust of the flesh. For the flesh lusteth against the Spirit, and the Spirit against the flesh: and these are contrary the one to the other: so that ye cannot do the things that ye would. But if ye be led of the Spirit, ye are not under the law.*
Galatians 5:24-25 *And they that are Christ's have crucified the flesh with the affections and lusts. If we live in the Spirit, let us also walk in the Spirit.*

Philippians 3:2-3 *Beware of dogs, beware of evil workers, beware of the concision. For we are the circumcision, which worship God in the spirit, and rejoice in Christ Jesus, and have no confidence in the flesh.*

John 6:63 *It is the spirit that quickeneth; the flesh profiteth nothing: the words that I speak unto you, they are spirit, and they are life.*

People must discern through the Holy Spirit only so they can provide factual insight of good and evil, right and wrong, holy and unholy, godly and demonic to others. They must be able to detect when there is demonic influence, hinderstands, oppressions, and possessions hindering a people's life, destiny, and vision.

Gifts of Healing – We discern that because the word says, "gifts of Healing," this gift manifests is immeasurable and unconventional ways. Let me be clear that these healing gifts align with the biblical principles, character, and nature of God. They do not include witchcraft, new age practices, or demonic workings. People can heal illnesses, minds, emotions, lands, spheres, dead visions. They heal the hope, ability, and perseverance in people. They may possess the healing gift of laying on of hands and may be deliverers who use what is in their hands – their life's visions - to heal people, regions, nations, and spheres of influence.

> **A Hebrew name of God is "Jehovah Raphah," meaning the God who heals**

Raphah also means:
1. to mend (by stitching), heal individual hurts
2. (figuratively) to cure, to (cause to) heal
3. to be healed by or likened unto a physician
4. to repair, thoroughly, make whole, make healthful
5. heal national defects and distresses or hurts, restore national favor

Exodus 15:26 *And said, If thou wilt diligently hearken to the voice of the Lord thy God, and wilt do that which is right in his sight, and wilt give ear to his commandments, and keep all his statutes, I will put none of these diseases upon thee, which I have brought upon the Egyptians: for I am the Lord that healeth thee.*

Deuteronomy 32:39 *See now that I, even I, am he, and there is no god with me: I kill, and I make alive; I wound, and I heal: neither is there any that can deliver out of my hand.*

2Chronicles 7:14 *If my people, which are called by my name, shall humble themselves, and pray, and seek my face, and turn from their wicked ways; then will I hear from heaven, and will forgive their sin, and will heal their land.*

Psalm 107:20 *He sent out His word and healed them, and delivered them from their destruction.*

Isaiah 53:5 *But He was pierced for our transgressions, He was crushed for our iniquities; the punishment that brought us peace was on Him, and by His wounds we are healed.*

A New Testament Greek Word for Healing is "Therapeuo"

Therapeuo means:
1. to wait upon menially
2. (figuratively) to adore (God), or (specially) to relieve (of disease)
3. to cure, heal, worship
4. to serve, do service, restore to health

Matthew 4:23 *And he went throughout all Galilee, teaching in their synagogues and proclaiming the gospel of the kingdom and healing every disease and every affliction among the people.*

Matthew 10:1 *And He called to Him His twelve disciples and gave them authority over unclean spirits, to cast them out, and to heal every disease and every affliction.*

Matthew 10:8 *Heal the sick, raise the dead, cleanse those who have leprosy, drive out demons. Freely you have received; freely give.*

1Peter 2:24 He personally bore our sins in His [own] body on the tree [as on an altar and offered Himself on it], that we might die (cease to exist) to sin and live to righteousness. By His wounds you have been healed.

3John 1:2 Dear friend, I pray that you may enjoy good health and that all may go well with you, even as your soul is getting along well.

Working of Miracles – People with this gift can be used by God to do any type of creative miracle, thus manifesting heaven in their sphere. There is no limit to what God can do. Such persons possess the ability and faith to believe God for anything.

The word *miracles* is *dunamis* in Greek and means:
1. force (literally or figuratively); specially, miraculous power (usually by implication, a miracle itself)
2. ability, abundance, meaning, might(-ily, -y, -y deed), (worker of) miracle(-s), power, strength
3. violence, mighty (wonderful) work, mighty work, strength, miracle, might, virtue
4. strength power, ability
    a) inherent power, power residing in a thing by virtue of its nature, or which a person or thing exerts and puts forth
    b) power for performing miracles
    c) moral power and excellence of soul
    d) the power and influence which belong to riches and wealth
    e) power and resources arising from numbers
    f) power consisting in or resting upon armies, forces

Matthew 19:26 Jesus looked at them and said, "With man this is impossible, but with God all things are possible.

Luke 1:37 For nothing is impossible with God.

Mark 9:23 If you can'?" said Jesus. "Everything is possible for him who believes.

Jeremiah 32:17 Ah, Sovereign LORD, you have made the heavens and the earth by your great power and outstretched arm. Nothing is too hard for you.
Romans 8:31 What, then, shall we say in response to this? If God is for us, who can be against us?

Job 42:2 "I know that you can do all things; no plan of yours can be thwarted.

John 14:11-13 Believe me that I am in the Father, and the Father in me: or else believe me for the very works' sake. Verily, verily, I say unto you, He that believeth on me, the works that I do shall he do also; and greater works than these shall he do; because I go unto my Father. And whatsoever ye shall ask in my name, that will I do, that the Father may be glorified in the Son.

Isaiah 46:10 I make known the end from the beginning, from ancient times, what is still to come. I say: My purpose will stand, and I will do all that I please.

Gift Of Administration - The gift of administration provides the ability to govern and manage clerical duties that aides in the organization of tasks operations, clerical and business endeavors.

Dictionary.com defines *administer* as:
verb (used with object):
1. to manage (affairs, a government, etc.); have executive charge of
2. to bring into use or operation
3. to make application of; give
4. to supervise the formal taking of (an oath or the like)
5. Law. to manage or dispose of, as a decedent's estate by an executor or administrator or a trust estate by a trustee

verb (used without object):
1. to contribute assistance; bring aid or supplies (usually followed by to)
2. to perform the duties of an administrator

Dictionary.com defines an *administrator* as:
1. a person who manages or has a talent for managing
2. Law. a person appointed by a court to take charge of the estate of a decedent, but not appointed in the decedent's will

The most common scripture known for administration is *1Corinthians 12:28* and actually called "*goverments*" in this passage of scripture.

1Corinthians 12:28 And God hath set some in the church, first apostles, secondarily prophets, thirdly teachers, after that miracles, then gifts of healings, helps, governments, diversities of tongues.

1Corinthians 12:28 New King James Bible And God has appointed these in the church: first apostles, second prophets, third teachers, after that miracles, then gifts of healings, helps, administrations, varieties of tongues.

Even if a person does not possess this gift, they will need to hire someone who can help them govern and manage ministerial, business, marketplace, or organizational endeavors. It is easier to have an administer taking care of these areas and not having to try and juggle so many tasks and positions. It is also best to have an administrator that can grow in relationship and vision with you so that they can develop a love and grace for you as their boss and for the vision God has given you. I say this because in the passage of scripture above we see that administrator is listed with gifts but also fivefold offices.

According to Strong's to *set* means:
1. to put, laydown, make, appoint, kneel down, to set on (serve) something
2. to set forth, something to be explained by discourse
3. to make (or set) for oneself or one's use, to set, fix establish, to set forth
4. to establish and to ordain, to place (in the widest application
5. literally and figuratively; properly, in a passive or horizontal posture), advise, bow, commit, conceive, and give

The gift of administration has a governmental officiating role that cannot be taken lightly as it can make or break a business organization, or ministry. When there is poor administration, a person can be awesome, however, the business will suffer. Clients may not get the paperwork or information they need on time, financials and tax documents can be misappropriated or misaligned, documents may not be properly utilized or filed, appointments can be missed, appointments can be missed or unscheduled. If the business is online and in person, this can posse an additional level of administrating that can be tedious, especially when factoring in flyers, advertising, etc. This is just a few administrative duties to consider.

It is important to hire someone who really have the heart and call of an administrator as these tasks should not be given to just anyone. So many people will claim to be able to do administrative work, but often they are just looking for a job and quick income. They do not recognize they are are actually governing someone's vision and business and their decisions or lack thereof can gravely impact the success or lack thereof regarding that business. Let's explore the meaning of administration (or governments in KJV) as well as helps in *1Corinthians 12:28*,

Strong's definition for *government* is *kybérnēsis*:
1. pilotage, i.e. (figuratively) directorship (in the church), government

Strong's definition of *helps* is *antílēpsis*:
1. relief, help
2. to take hold of in turn, i.e. succor; also to participate:—help, partaker, support

The gift of administration and the gift of helps become intertwined when one is an administrator, but the assignments are different. One who has the gift of helps is not always one who is an administrator. The gift of helps is to assist with relief, aid, and assistance, while the purpose of an administrator is to aide and uphold the vision so that the foundation is solid, but also to make sure helpers are in place to sustain and maintain the business. Ask God to reveal to you what type of administrator you need. Then begin to interview and pursue what he is showing you. Make sure that person can do more than just general clerical duties. Make sure they understand and is confident in LLC requirements, business tax documents, business software, due dates for the business being in order, hiring helpers to aide the business. Empower them so that they have God's eyes for your vision and can help you steward properly what God has grant to your hands. Pay them properly and even as they are with you for years, give them a financial stock in your company to bless the inheritance to which they have invested in your business.

Governmental Offices - Fivefold ministry offices are ordained positions that disciples, trains, equipes, officiates governmental legislation through the kingdom of heaven so that God's kingdom can be established and advanced in the earth. For detailed revelation of the fivefold offices, please purchase my *"Fivefold Operations Volume I manual."*

Ephesians 4:11
• Apostle • Prophet • Evangelist • Pastor • Teacher

Ephesians 4:11-13 And he gave some, apostles; and some, prophets; and some, evangelists; and some, pastors and teachers; For the perfecting of the saints, for the work of the ministry, for the edifying of the body of Christ: Till we all come in the unity of the faith, and of the knowledge of the Son of God, unto a perfect man, unto the measure of the stature of the fulness of Christ.

This passage of scripture presents the relevancy of purpose for Jesus, giving the gifts of the fivefold offices to the church. Jesus never took these gifts away. He would never give a gift then take it back. These gifts are just as important today as they were over 2,000 years ago. When Jesus gave these gifted offices, it was for:

✓ The perfecting and maturing of God's people, his church, the community, lands, and regions.

- ✓ The work and equipping of the ministry where the church and the world would come to God for assistance and supply of their needs and desires.
- ✓ The edifying, empowering, building up of the Body of Christ.

This was to be continual until solidification:

- ✓ In the faith and of the knowledge of the Son of God was evident.
- ✓ Of the full maturity and growth in the Lord was a tangible lifestyle.
- ✓ Where all reached the full measure of the stature of Christ.

This mandate reveals that fivefold ministry is never-ending. It is the purpose of God for the saints and for his church. It is the revival reformation that we are to be manifesting, releasing, and establishing in the earth. SHIFT!

God installs these offices in his chosen at birth. If he does not install this office in you, you cannot promote yourself to this office or go to a Christian school, learn these gifts, then be positioned into these offices. Either they are in you or they are not. Either they are part of your destiny and calling or not. These offices are for the purposes of providing spiritual authorities that can empower, equip, and release the body of Christ in their giftings and callings while asserting and maintaining Godly jurisdiction against principalities and strongholds that would strive to bind people, lands, and regions. A person can be apostolic, prophetic, evangelistic, etc., but not operate in a governmental office. The office provides the officer the ability to govern and legislate against demonic entities, spiritual realms, regions, and within the constructs of assemblies, businesses, and communities. If God has not called you to this, you can encounter a lot of hardship and tribulation by putting yourself in these positions as those who have the offices, have a grace to contend and endure the warfare that comes with these offices.

2Corinthians 4:8-17 We are troubled on every side, yet not distressed; we are perplexed, but not in despair; Persecuted, but not forsaken; cast down, but not destroyed; Always bearing about in the body the dying of the Lord Jesus, that the life also of Jesus might be made manifest in our body. For we which live are always delivered unto death for Jesus' sake, that the life also of Jesus might be made manifest in our mortal flesh. So then death worketh in us, but life in you.

We having the same spirit of faith, according as it is written, I believed, and therefore have I spoken; we also believe, and therefore speak; Knowing that he which raised up the Lord Jesus shall raise up us also by Jesus, and shall present us with you. For all things are for your sakes, that the abundant grace might through the thanksgiving of many redound to the glory of God. For which cause we faint not; but though our outward man perish, yet the inward man is renewed day by day. For our light affliction, which is but for a moment, worketh for us a far more exceeding and eternal weight of glory; While we look not at the things which are seen, but at the things which are not seen: for the things which are seen are temporal; but the things which are not seen are eternal.

Though as saints, we endure some of this for the gospel's sake, those in governmental offices live this daily as a lifestyle and mandate. It can be a constant spiritual and natural battle depending on what season of destiny they are in. Imagine striving to endure this type of lifestyle warfare daily without God creating you for this position? It would be a horrific life of unnecessary hardship.

I also want to say that if God called you to these offices and you do not embrace them, you can have warfare. The principalities and powers in these jurisdictions are contending and waring for these realms and you will feel and experience the weight of that whether you embrace your gifted office or not. Your ability to contend and tower in the grace God has given you over these entities is to SHIFT into your rightful office and establish the authority God has given you to govern over darkness within your spheres of influences.

Learn about all the fivefold ministry offices so you can walk in them if God has called you to government seats. Seek training and equipping if you called to an office. Fivefold officers are able to govern over the lives, visions, and spheres that they are called to at a distinct authoritative dimension. Your fivefold office will give you the authority to push back darkness, combat evil, infiltrate and judge systems, and overthrow principalities and powers.

It is possible to be called of God to operate in dual fivefold ministry offices. Sometimes you may start your ministry off in one seat and God will reveal the other seat as he expands your ministry and purpose. Or you may have seasons of switching in and out of fivefold ministry seats. The key to recognizing if you are operating in an office or just an anointing well is if you actually GOVERN AS AN OFFICER in those seasons or moments God is using you in those seats. Many assume works, signs, and wonders validate that they are ready for the office. But the office is more than just ministry, labor, and gift manifestations. This is the work of a believer, but not necessarily the government of the office.

Some officer duties include:

- Leading platoons (e.g., a company or groups of people, a military unit, team, headquarters).
- Counseling and mentoring people and releasing and journeying with them in their destiny and calling.
- Teaching, training, and equipping new, low ranking, or specialized officers, or groups of people that God has charged oversight to.
- Incur the maintenance, integration, management, and administration of the office.
- Commanding troops during war.

- Sustaining and maintaining critical military operations.
- Contending against high ranking demonic and or wicked officers.
- Overseeing ministries, market place, and business arenas, social and community organizations, and political or economic liaisons.
- Overseeing communities, regions, or nations.

When one is in the office, all authority is given unto them in heaven and in earth.

> *Matthew 18:16 Then the eleven disciples went away into Galilee, into a mountain where Jesus had appointed them. And when they saw him, they worshipped him: but some doubted. And Jesus came and spake unto them, saying, All power is given unto me in heaven and in earth.*

This means the officer's authority is without measure. They have been ordained by God to reign and rule in both spheres such that the kingdom of God is evident in all they set their hands to do. SHIFT!

Sevenfold Spirit Of The Lord

In addition to being born with talents and gifts, born in gifted offices, and pursuing supernatural gifts, the Spirit of the Lord can rest upon you with an anointing and qualification to judge through the intellect and mind of God.

> *Isaiah 11:2 And the spirit of the Lord shall rest upon him, the spirit of wisdom and understanding, the spirit of counsel and might, the spirit of knowledge and of the fear of the Lord. And shall make him of quick understanding in the fear of the Lord: and he shall not judge after the sight of his eyes, neither reprove after the hearing of his ears: But with righteousness shall he judge the poor, and reprove with equity for the meek of the earth: and he shall smite the earth: with the rod of his mouth, and with the breath of his lips shall he slay the wicked.*

Gifts Make Room

Proverbs 18:12 says, "A man's gift maketh room for him, and bringeth him before great men."

We tend to equate this scripture to our capabilities and talents. However, the word *gift* in this scripture means, "*offerings, presents, reward, gift.*" This revelation lets us know that when we give our gifts as a blessing to others, our works make room for us and SHIFTS us into greatness. This is essential to recognizing that our gifts and talents have purpose. They are to empower someone's life, the earth, and the world at large. We must pursue

God for how he desires us to impact others, the earth, and the world, so we can be the greatest person he desired us to be. SHIFT!

Calling Activation:

1. Spend time with God assessing and journaling your gifts and the calling?

   - What spiritual gifts you possess?
   - What is your callings?
   - Journal your understanding of officiating in an office.
   - What fivefold ministerial office/s do you possess?
   - How do you know you are called to this officiating fivefold seat?
   - What has God spoken to you regarding operating in this office?
   - How are they vital to your calling? Be mindful of and include in your journal entry the following considerations: your life experiences, successes and failures, how you engage, interact, and impact people, group settings, team assignments, environments, lands, communities, and spheres as this can reveal a lot about what you gifts, wells, callings, purposes, and/or fivefold ministry office may be.

2. What gifts and spiritual attributes as it relates to this chapter do you need to mature in to strengthen your calling?

3. What areas in your behaviors, character, interactions with people, how you handle the matters of God, do you need to mature in to help strengthen your calling?

4. What has God said or shown you in a vision or dream about how your gifts will expand and make room for you?

5. What do you need to submit to, commit to, be accountable to, such that you consistently use your gifts so they can make room for you?

6. Ask God to give you a love to live sold out and consecrated inside his prayer watch tower. Journal strategic goals and plans you can implement to be rooted and grounded in who you are and what you are to do for God.

Live In The Shift!

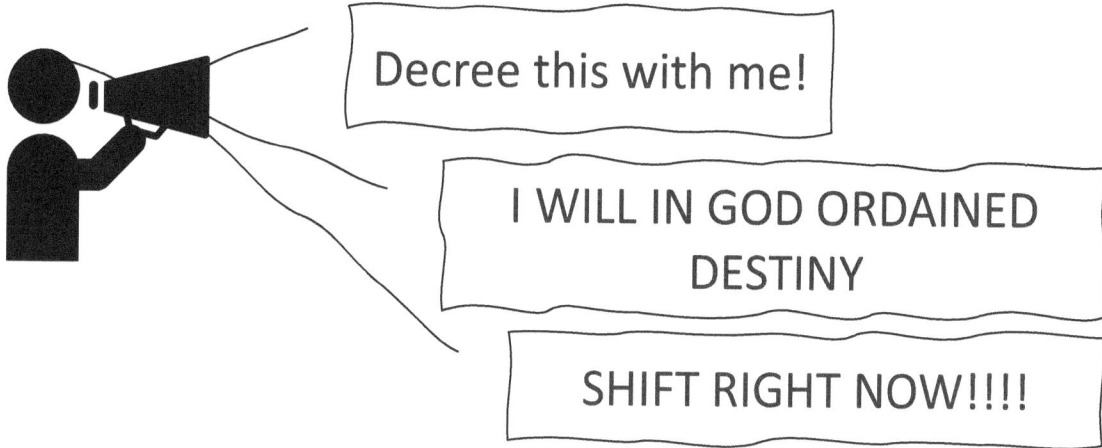

RESOURCES

Books by Dr. Taquetta Baker

Discerning God's Voice By Taquetta Baker
Kingdom Wellness Counseling & Mentoring Manual Volume I By Taquetta Baker
Sustaining The Vision Workbook by Taquetta Baker

Websites

Blueletterbible.com
Biblestudytools.com
Dictionary.com
Olivetree.com
Strong's Exhaustive Bible Concordance Online Bible Study Tools

Shift right now!

Be a Healthy You!

Kingdom Shifters Product Line

Products available at kingdomshiftingbooks.com and amazon.com	
Books (Paperback, Kindle, and e-books available)	
Healing the Wounded Leader	There is an App for That
Apostolic Governing	Sustaining The Vision Workbook
Apostolic Mantle	Annihilating Church Hurt
Healing the Wounded Leader	Discerning the Voice of God
Release the Vision	Feasting in His Presence
Birthing Books That Shift Generations	Prayers that Shift Atmospheres
Atmosphere Changes (Weaponry)	Dismantling Homosexuality
Strategies for Eradicating Racism	Let There Be Sight
Kingdom Shifters Decree That Thang	Kingdom Watchman Builder on the Wall
Kingdom Heirs Decree That Thang	Kingdom Keys to Governing Relationships
Fivefold Operations – Manuals I, II, and III	Unmasking the Power of the Scouts – Volumes I and II
Processing Grief & Loss	Cultivating Destiny From The Womb
Kingdom Wellness Counseling & Mentoring Manual I	Deliverance From The Stronghold of Suicide
Truth About Willful Sin	Ascending Into Heavenly Realms
Gatekeeping Regions For God's Glory	KW Life Coaching Manual
The Power Of Purity	Deliverance Is The Children's Bread Volume I & II
Books for Liturgical / Interpretive Dance Ministries	
Dance & Fivefold Ministry	Dance from Heaven to Earth
Spirits that Attack Dance Ministers	Dancers! Dancers! Dancers! Decree That Thang
CD's	
Decree That Thang	Kingdom Heirs Decree That Thang
Teaching and Worship	

www.ingramcontent.com/pod-product-compliance
Lightning Source LLC
Chambersburg PA
CBHW081638040426

42449CB00014B/3372